Deleted

© 2022 Sunbird Books, an imprint of Phoenix International Publications, Inc.
8501 West Higgins Road   59 Gloucester Place   Heimhuder Straße 81
Chicago, Illinois 60631   London W1U 8JJ   20148 Hamburg

www.sunbirdkidsbooks.com

Sunbird Books and the colophon are trademarks of Phoenix International Publications, Inc.

Library of Congress Control Number: 2021936151

ISBN: 978-1-5037-6007-3 Printed in China

The art for this book was created digitally.
Text is set in Filson Pro.

IT'S HER STORY
DOLLY PARTON

Written by Emily Skwish
Illustrated by Lidia Fernández Abril

sunbird books

Bright lights, rhinestones, costume changes, jokes, stories, and music... **Dolly Parton** is on the stage!

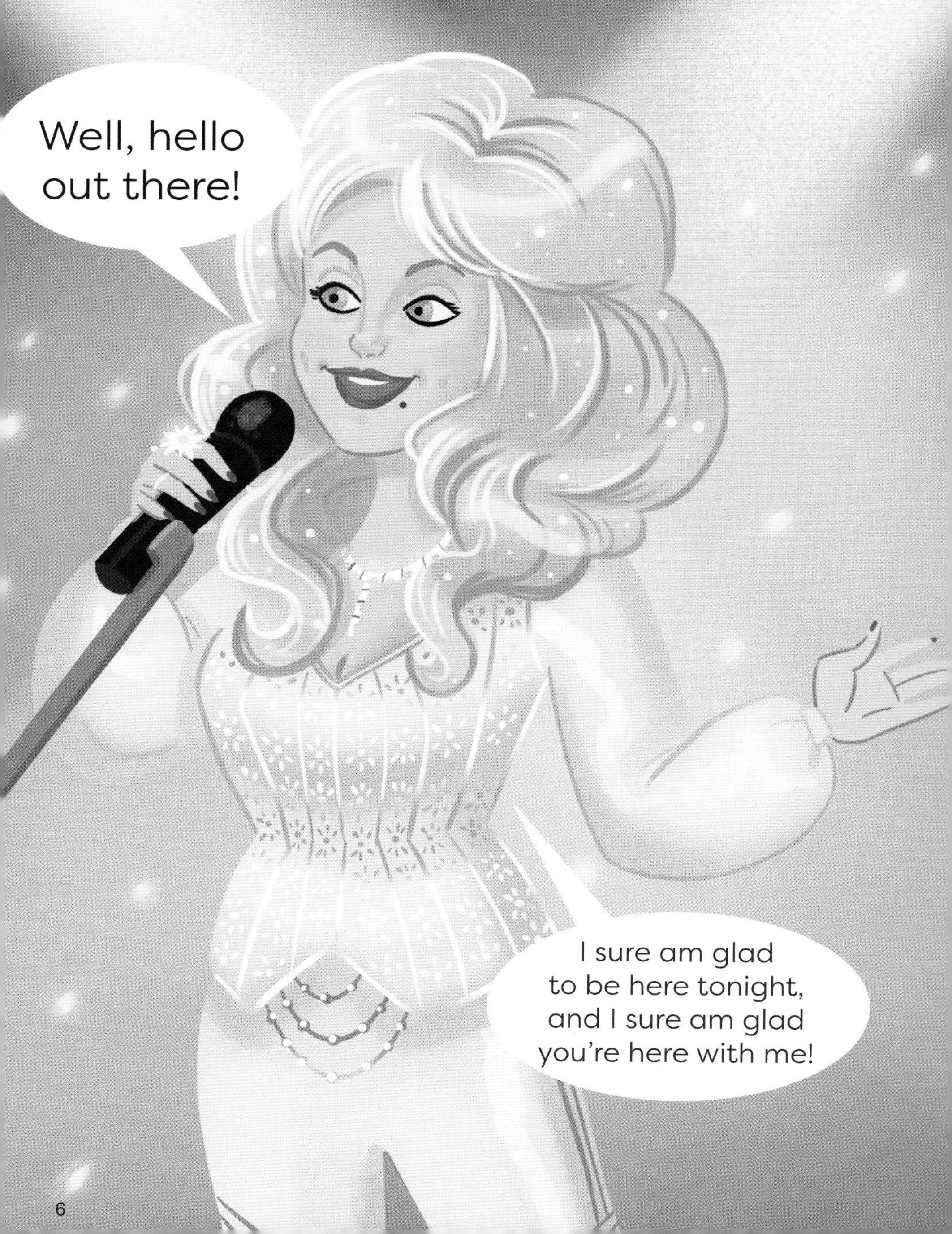
Well, hello out there!
I sure am glad to be here tonight, and I sure am glad you're here with me!

Dolly doesn't just entertain—she brings people together. The folks in the audience all have one thing in common:

Her story starts far away from the bright lights of the stage.

Dolly was born on January 19th, 1946, in Sevierville, Tennessee, in the foothills of the Great Smoky Mountains. Dolly's father had to ride a horse to bring the doctor to the house.

Dolly's parents, Lee and Avie Lee Parton, didn't have any money to pay the doctor.

Waaaaah!

They paid with a sack of cornmeal.

Dolly was Lee and Avie Lee's fourth child, and the family kept growing and growing.

Hi!

The house had no electricity, no running water, and no indoor bathroom. Money was always tight...

...so the family found creative ways to fix up a bare wall or make toys and clothes out of things they saved around the house.

Avie Lee loved to sing, and so did Dolly.

Dolly also loved to rhyme. When she was five years old, she wrote her very first song. It was about her corn cob doll.

Avie Lee was so proud of Dolly's songwriting!

Come hear the song this little thing wrote!

Avie Lee wrote down the words to Dolly's songs. She knew that Dolly would want to look back at them someday.

Lee Parton was a big fan of the Grand Ole Opry, a country music variety show broadcast from Nashville.

The family would gather around to listen...whenever they could get their radio to work.

Dolly dreamed of a life in music, and it wasn't long before she was performing in front of big audiences...

Y'all listenin'?

of chickens, or whoever was around to hear her sing into her tin can microphone, imagining herself on stage at the Grand Ole Opry.

Dolly loved to read, but she didn't like going to school. She wanted to be singing and writing instead!

...I bet I could even get paid to sing my songs. What if they gave me five dollars? I'd be rich! And then...

Plus, the other kids at school could be mean.

This is like the coat of many colors Joseph wore in the Bible.

It's beautiful!

My mama made me a new coat!

Ain't it pretty?

Later, Dolly would write a song and a picture book about the experience. Schools use the story to help stop bullying.

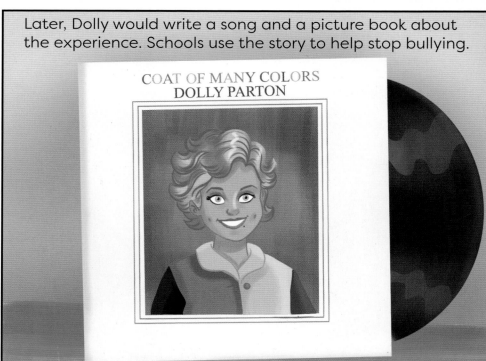

When Dolly was ten, her Uncle Bill helped her get a spot performing on the Cas Walker radio show in Knoxville!

It was Dolly's first time in the spotlight...and she sparkled!

Three years later, her dream came true. A Grand Ole Opry performer let Dolly take his place!

We've got a little girl here from up in East Tennessee...let's bring her out here!

By golly, **Johnny Cash** is a-talkin' about me!

The audience loved her.

They keep clappin'! What do I do?

Well, just play it again!

She played "**You Gotta Be My Baby**" three times!

As a teenager, Dolly traveled back and forth to Knoxville to perform on the Cas Walker show.

Her Uncle Bill and other friends and family helped her get to the studio.

Her hairstyle changed...

and her performances got better and better!

At her high school graduation, Dolly and her classmates all had to stand up and tell the others their plans.

Everyone laughed at her! But that just made Dolly more determined than ever.

The next day, Dolly headed to Nashville.

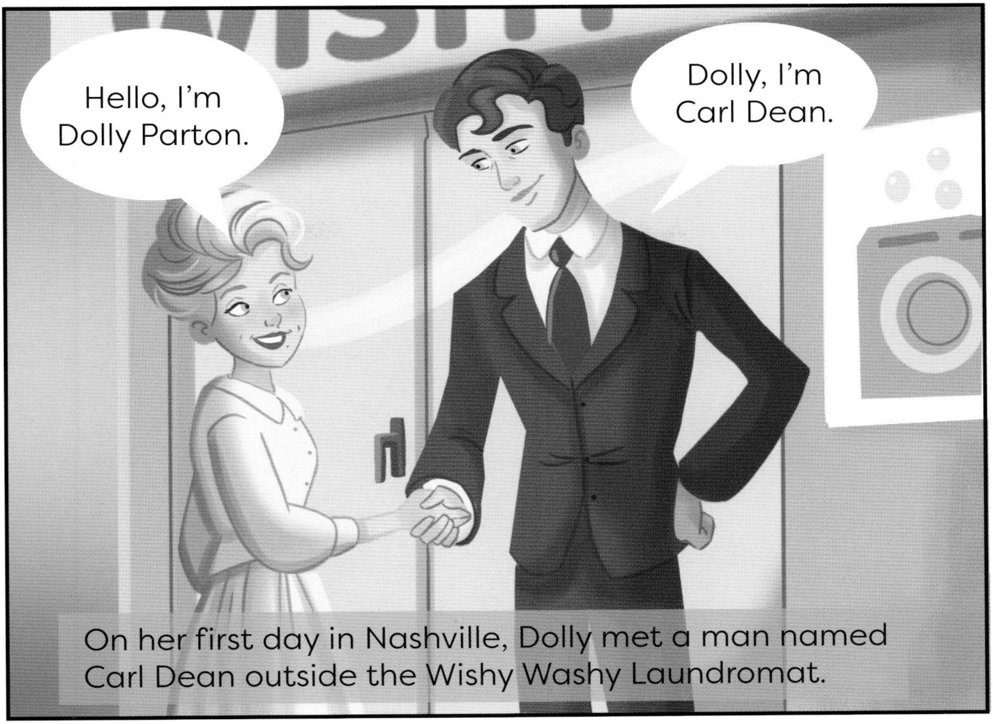
Hello, I'm Dolly Parton.
Dolly, I'm Carl Dean.
On her first day in Nashville, Dolly met a man named Carl Dean outside the Wishy Washy Laundromat.

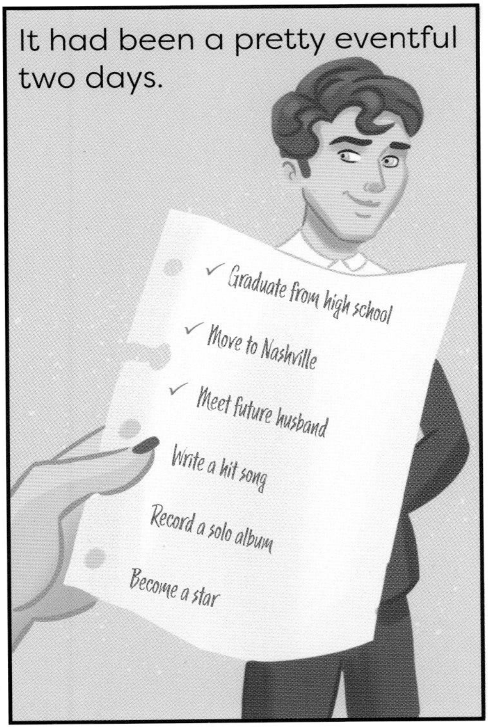
It had been a pretty eventful two days.
✓ Graduate from high school
✓ Move to Nashville
✓ Meet future husband
Write a hit song
Record a solo album
Become a star

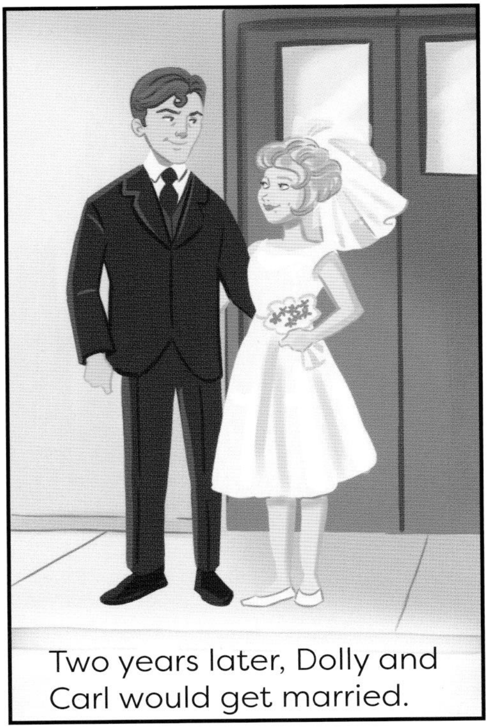
Two years later, Dolly and Carl would get married.

During those early days in Nashville, Dolly didn't have a lot of money. When it came to finding something to eat, she had to get creative.

But Dolly kept writing, and soon, she was writing songs for Nashville stars like Bill Phillips...

You need another hit song, Bill? 'Cause I got lots more.

Just wait'll you hear this one here...

and her idol, Kitty Wells.

You sing so pretty, Kitty!

Dolly wrote songs about things that had happened to her, and about things she made up.

She wrote sad songs, too.

It's about a woman, a man...

"...and a dog, and all they have is the rags on their backs..."

"Or this one about going to bed hungry, in the good old days...when times were bad!"

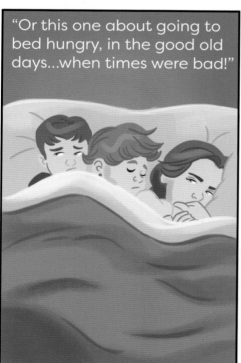

These songs let Dolly connect with all kinds of people.

Dolly had success writing songs for *other* people to sing, but most record executives thought her voice was too unusual to record her own album.

25

After three years in Nashville, she finally got to record an album of her own! And it was a hit!

Dolly's album caught the attention of Porter Wagoner. He was a country music star. He had his own traveling act. He even had his own TV show!

Porter hired Dolly to replace a singer named Norma Jean.

Pretty Miss Dolly Parton!

That's right, I sound pretty, too! Wait'll they hear me sing...

Audiences loved Norma Jean and her low, rich singing voice. When Dolly began to sing in her high, clear voice, the audience was shocked.

Why's her voice so high?

She's no Norma Jean!

Later, things got worse... the audience booed!

BOO!

BOO!

BOO!

BOO!

Y'all need to get some manners!

Dolly was sad. She had worked so hard to get here! But she believed in herself and didn't give up.

Porter believed in Dolly, too. They began performing duets—romantic songs about love, and funny songs that sounded like arguments.

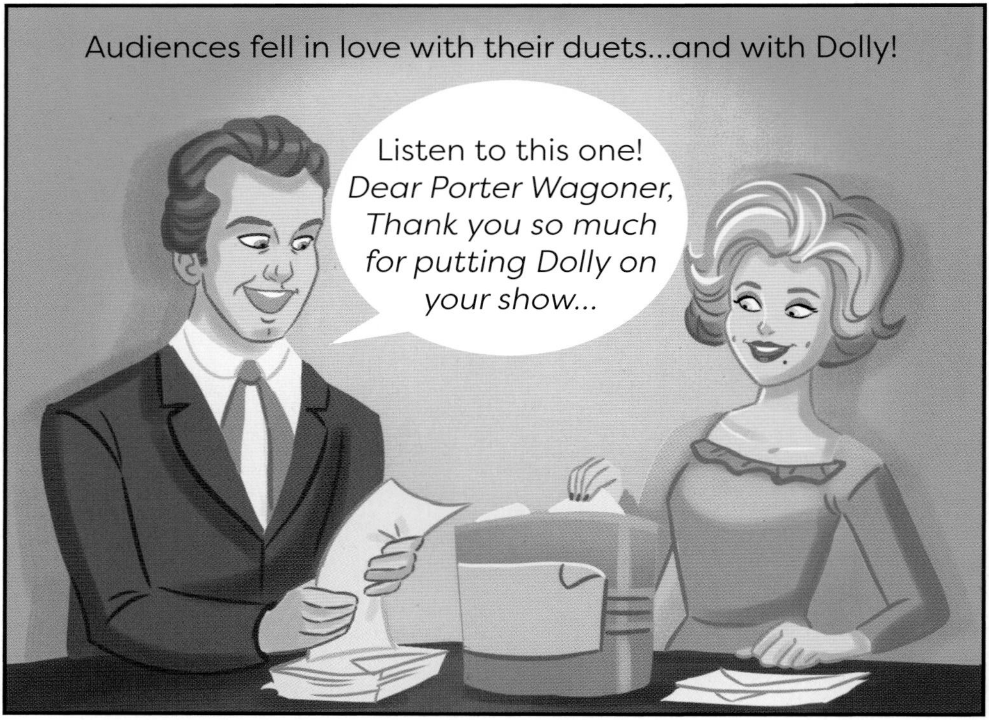
Audiences fell in love with their duets...and with Dolly!
Listen to this one! *Dear Porter Wagoner, Thank you so much for putting Dolly on your show...*

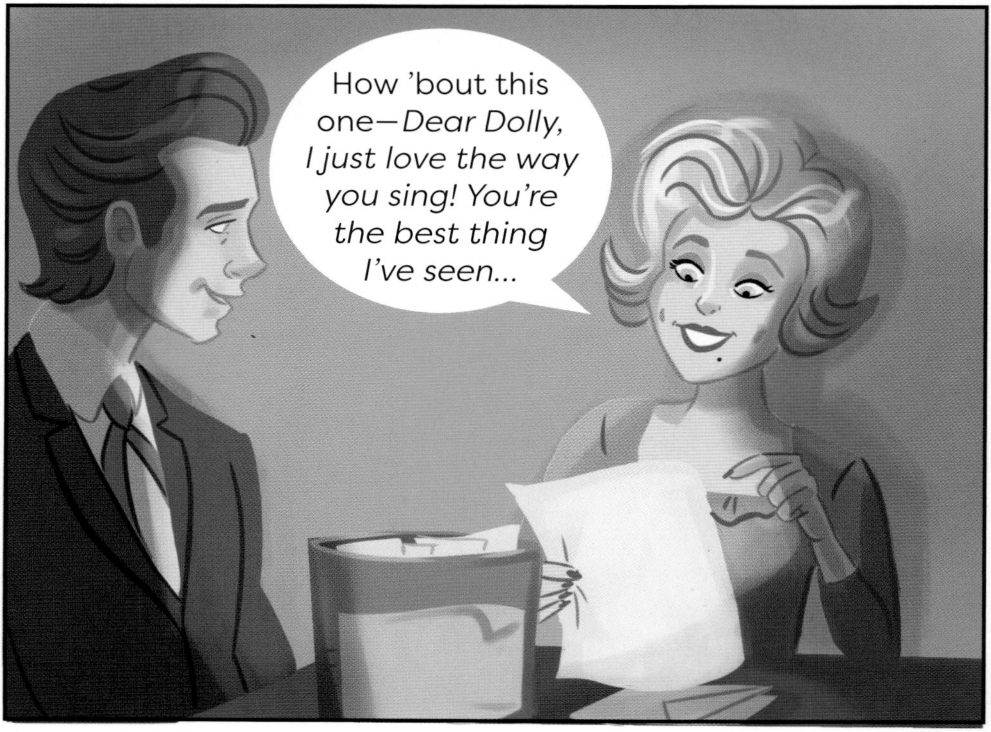
How 'bout this one—*Dear Dolly, I just love the way you sing! You're the best thing I've seen...*

But as time went on, Porter and Dolly didn't just argue in their songs. They argued in real life. Porter wanted to control everything Dolly did.

Dolly had to spend a lot of time standing up to Porter...

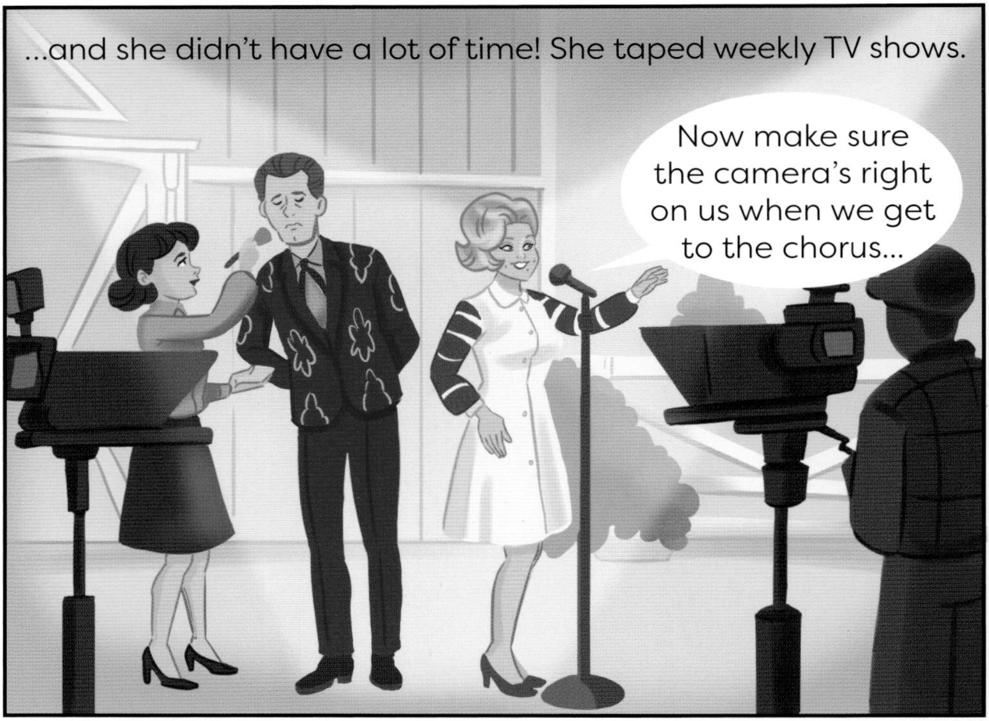
...and she didn't have a lot of time! She taped weekly TV shows.
Now make sure the camera's right on us when we get to the chorus...

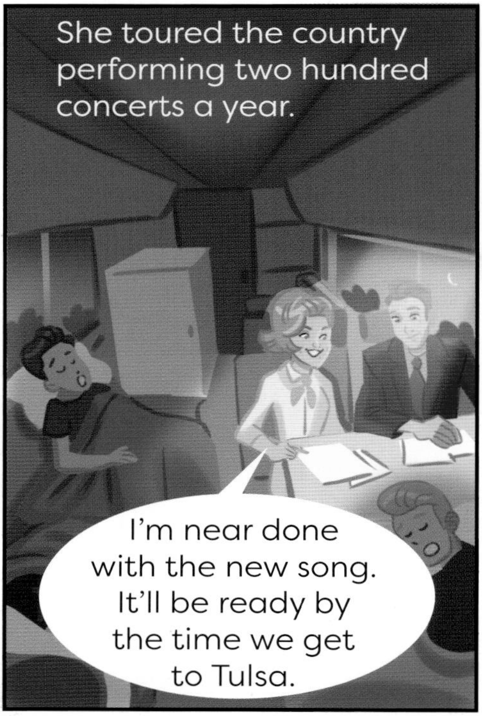
She toured the country performing two hundred concerts a year.
I'm near done with the new song. It'll be ready by the time we get to Tulsa.

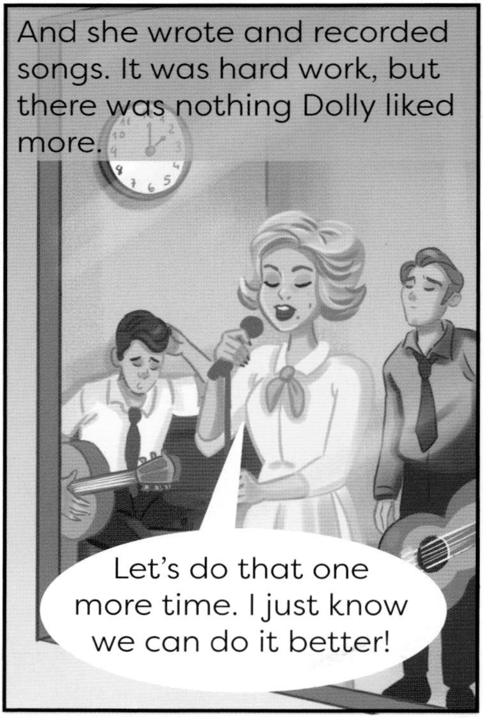
And she wrote and recorded songs. It was hard work, but there was nothing Dolly liked more.
Let's do that one more time. I just know we can do it better!

There were lots of fun, exciting times, too! In 1969, Dolly became a member of the Grand Ole Opry.

She knew her parents were listening at home. They were so proud of her!

33

After seven years with Porter Wagoner, Dolly knew she had to move on. Porter was angry, but Dolly felt free! She was ready to try new things and work with new people.

Through the next 40 years, Dolly worked hard and in new ways. She was ready to try everything...

I'm not going to limit myself.

from movies...

Hollywood, here I am!

to television (her OWN show this time)...

We're gonna have a lot of fun! Let's show 'em what we mean...

to pop songs!

Some of Dolly's fans weren't ready for her new adventures.

I'm not leaving country. I'm just taking it with me!

Soon, Dolly had more fans than ever—country fans, pop fans, movie fans, fans who loved her sparkly clothes...and her even sparklier personality.

It's hard to be a diamond in a rhinestone world!

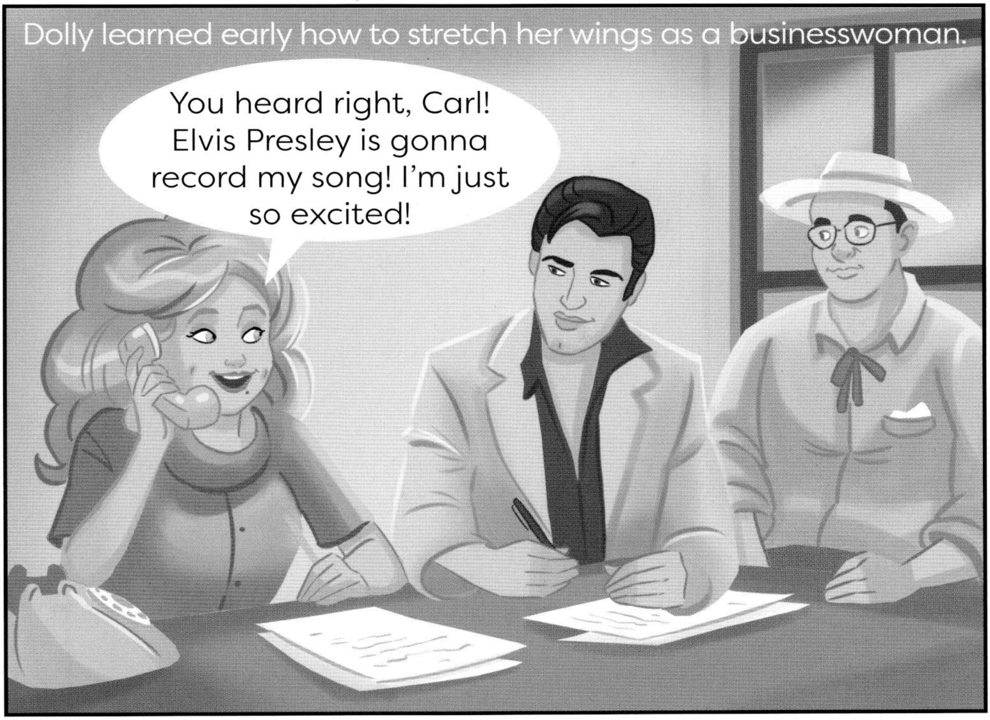
Dolly learned early how to stretch her wings as a businesswoman.
You heard right, Carl! Elvis Presley is gonna record my song! I'm just so excited!

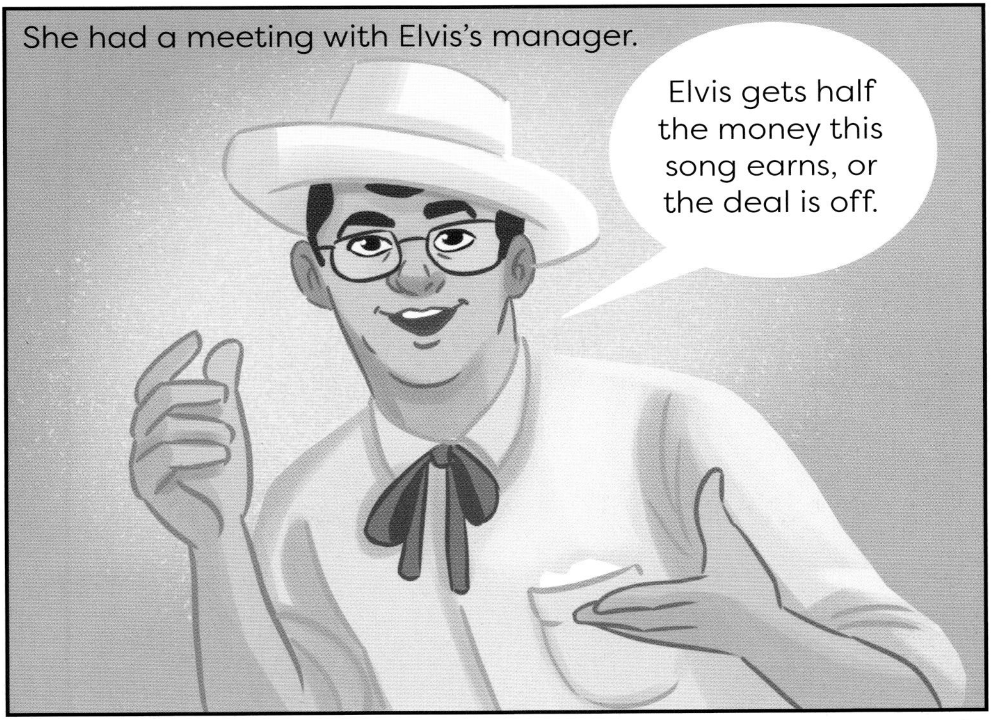
She had a meeting with Elvis's manager.
Elvis gets half the money this song earns, or the deal is off.

So if anyone recorded the song in the future, Elvis would get half the money.

I really want Elvis to record my song, but that doesn't seem fair...

Well, I'm sorry, then the deal is off.

It was a smart decision. Eighteen years later, Whitney Houston recorded "I Will Always Love You." It was a worldwide hit, and Dolly earned millions of dollars!

Another smart business move was opening Dollywood, a theme park in Pigeon Forge, Tennessee, right near where Dolly grew up.

Dollywood employs four thousand people and brings millions of dollars to the area every year.

Music, jobs, butterflies— Dollywood's got everything!

Bringing money into the community is just one way Dolly helps others. Her Imagination Library project gives children a free book every month from the time they're born until they begin school.

Once upon a time, there was a little girl with a big dream...

She created the library to honor her dad, who never learned to read or write.

Even though Dolly's high school graduation isn't her happiest memory, she believes education is important.

I made it! Gimme that diploma, then Nashville, here I come!

Dolly created the Buddy Program to encourage students to finish high school, giving them five hundred dollars when they graduated. And she gives thousands of dollars each year to help students pay for college.

You made it! Now, find out who you are, and do it on purpose!

Although Dolly never went to college, she received an honorary degree from the University of Tennessee.

If I had but one wish for you, it would be for you to dream more.

Dreams build convictions because you work hard to pay the price to make sure that they come true!

Years ago, Dolly's big dreams helped make her a star.

Now, they help make a big difference in the world. In 2020, Dolly gave one million dollars to Vanderbilt University to help create a vaccine for Covid-19.

Be safe, be respectful, wear your mask, lead with love.

Wherever she goes, Dolly connects people who don't seem to have much in common...

except their ability to dream.

Emily Skwish loves to write about superheroes, so she was especially excited to write about real-life superhero Dolly! She lives in Evanston, Illinois, with her talented husband and two funny kids, and can often be heard singing "Jolene" as she goes about her day.

Lidia Fernández Abril started her career at different animation studios working as an inbetweener, clean-up artist, and storyboard artist. Now she focuses on illustrating children's books and comics, as well as designing characters and backgrounds for kids' games. She loves the process of developing a story, but what she enjoys most about her work is that it allows her to preserve her inner child and keep drawing! She lives in Valladolid, Spain, with her loved ones.